This book is dedicated to all the mothers of God's special Sons and Daughters who have spent their life on Earth without their children.

Your children are not lost, they are WAITING.

LUKE 2:19

"But Mary kept all these things, and pondered them in her heart." KJV

ROSES

Caroline Richardson

"In all the history of time,

A mama is chasing the fires of life,

Strong and soft and wide awake,

She's praying, all your troubles away."

-Chorus from *"It Takes A Mama"*

Music and Lyrics written by Caroline Richardson

ORDER OF EVENTS

WHY ROSES

My Eli….

In my early twenties I married, had a beautiful son by my first husband, and experienced divorce all before I was 26. I had finally gotten my head up above the sinking waters of life and then the tsunami came that almost sunk my ship.

Being divorced and single at 26 is not a desirable position to be in. Divorce is shameful enough, let alone having to muster up the courage to try again at such a young age. No one ever wants to face that designation but there I was, and facing it was the only choice I had. Living in a small town where everyone knew everybody was the gas on the flame to my already out of hand fire. Divorce is just like death, except it does not die, it just walks around and taunts you. Facing defeat takes a courage only found in Jesus. There have been many days where I wanted to move permanently into my closet, and hide in the corner but we all know that life must go on and hiding never solves anything. Regardless of how you feel, life keeps moving, and you must move with it.

Nothing prepared me to be a divorced, single mother at 26 years old. I had failed miserably at marriage and everyone was watching. I felt like a soldier coming up out of a trench facing one million bullets face first. I made plenty of mistakes and this was one of the hardest seasons of my life.

After some time, I met a beautiful man that I deeply loved. A kind, compassionate soul that the world did not deserve. He was not afraid to ask hard things, had a loving way of listening, and never passed judgement. He too, had seen some fire in his own life, and the trials he had faced made him that much softer. We found great friendship together and laughter healed our broken hearts. I am a better person today for knowing him. We made lots of plans, and for the first time in a long time we were both very happy.

I remember where I was when I got the call. You do not forget things like that. It is like a bullet going through you and your unable to move. The why and how is not important when people are dead. It is just an empty feeling of helplessness that sears into your heart. Suddenly, Heaven is really real, and you are faced with hard questions in your heart that only God can answer. You think death is something far off in the future and then you are reminded of just how fragile our life is.

There really are no words that can describe the loss of a loved one. Only Jesus can comprehend the depth of that kind of pain.

When you experience the passing of a loved one, it changes you, and it certainly did me. The hard truth was this: I would never be the same. Facing yet another catastrophe, I was another year older on the outside, but I had aged a lifetime in my heart. I had lost another life in my heart to death. We create lives in our hearts, consisting of dreams, hopes, and plans. However, when they die, we still must live. We live in a world full of mean people. If you find yourself with dead dreams in your heart; give yourself grace in the season of pain. Those around you cannot see your scars, and you cannot expect them to. This is why you must cling to Jesus. God is the only one who can go deep in your heart and touch your pain; no one else can. Over time, Jesus sows' new dreams in our hearts and waters them to make them grow. For the life of the believer, He makes all things NEW (Revelation 21)

At this point I was all but hanging by a thread, and the thread was the hem of Jesus's garment. Much like the woman with the issue of blood, (Mark 5) I had issues too hard for other people to touch and became very isolated from the public and had to withdraw with Jesus.

The grass had not grown over the grave of death when I faced another hardship of life. I was pregnant, and unaware. In just a few short weeks, I had outlived another dream to death. A child that would have been so loved and wanted. I was the surviving factor in all these situations but I felt dead. There was no life in me left. To be so young, I felt so old. If I had not been a believer, with a strong faith in God, I think I would have died from a broken heart.

This is where my story turns from death- to life. Jesus promises us in John 14:18 these words, **"I will not leave you as orphans; I will come to you." (NIV).** Jesus came to me through the precious Holy Spirit, and showed me His promises before my spiritual eyes. I had been very early in my pregnancy at the time of miscarriage, and there was no way to know what the gender of the baby was. I had prayed and asked God to show me my baby. Daily, I went to the word of God and turned the noise of the earthly world off. In the word of God, I found peace and assurance and ultimately strength to keep living. I began having visions of Heaven. Out of nowhere, and all at once Heaven started coming down and downloading in my spirit. In a series of visions of Heaven, He not only showed me my baby, but I was able to see my baby with his father *enjoying Heaven*. It was a double fold blessing. Suddenly, the pain of losing them, became peace and joy as Heaven and the beautiful life they were living unfolded before me. Even though these dreams had died, God made them come alive again in my heart like only He can. I had many visions of not just my baby and his father, but also other family members that were in Heaven with them. Looking back, ***God truly opened the Heavens for me for many months, and kept coming back with reports of joy and not death***. I saw eternity and what it meant for the believer in Jesus Christ, and that is the strength that I am still living on today. For months, God through The Holy Spirit, would visit with me and pull back the curtain of Heaven and let me visit with them. This continued for a time, and then slowly the visions stopped coming. Since that time, I have continued to have visions of Heaven, but not the same way that I did after they died. God shared with me that my baby's name was Eli. This was his name that God had given him. A precious little boy.

God is faithful to us in our human state. He is faithful when we are hurting, and when we are angry. He is faithful when we do not understand, and when hard things come our way. He is constant in the life of His children guiding them and holding them up out of the **"the valley of death" (Psalm 23).**

I knew that God had a plan for the visions He had shown me; when I was walking through that season, I had a deep knowing that I was walking in a season I had not lived through yet. It was as if the things He was revealing to me were years ahead and I was behind seeing them from a time of rest. ***I also knew that there would be a time for me to give the visions back to Him in a way that He would be honored. God comforted me and gave me a beautiful gift, but there would come a time where I would be strong enough to give it back to Him with a joyful heart. Not in my own strength, but in His.***

Time is in His hand. He knows what we can handle, and what we cannot, and when we are strong enough to get up. Just like Jesus came to the invalid man beside the pool of Bethesda who had laid there for years, because of physical limitations, He came and attended to pain in my life that I had carried for years. Just like the man beside the pool, I too had made many attempts to rescue myself, and failed. During that season, Jesus had compassion on me, just like he did that invalid man. He comforted me and gave me peace. I too was laying in sorrow, and ***it was time to get up and live.*** Jesus speaks to years of pain and sorrow in a way that requires action in John 5:8; ***"Then Jesus said to him, "Get up! Pick up your mat and walk." NIV.*** The man was not healed in his own strength; but when Jesus spoke life over his body, it erased and eradicated years of suffering and gave him a chance to go on living and declare the good works of the Lord for others. ***When we get up as believers, we are giving Jesus the credit. We are showing the world, that Jesus's power is still alive on the earth thousands of years after He went to Heaven.*** Because, "He lives, we can live too" (John 14:19).

 It was the strength of God that lifted that man, and that lifts you and I.

The mission of Jesus was to extend Heaven to everyone He encountered in hopes that they too would see and believe and spend eternity with Him and His Father God. My friend, that is our mission as well. We can either sit in sorrow, or soar in grace.

I have always had a tender heart for women who have experienced abortion. I have always believed that life began at conception, and God was the creator of all life. After seeing all those visions of my own son in Heaven, it softened my heart even more for women who had experienced the loss of a child. One day I was laying in the sun praying and listening to stories of women who had experienced abortions. They were filled with pain, regret, and fear. As I listened to their stories, they all stated they hoped their baby had made it to Heaven. The next thing they all stated was they hoped their baby was not mad at them. The pain in their voice hit me deeper that day. I also watched a video, of an outreach that helped women overcome the pain of loss and abortion by giving them a way to honor their babies. This encouraged my spirit and turned the light switch on in my closet of blessings that God had given to me. I began thinking of all the visions I was given of my own son, and I started to feel guilty that I had seen all these beautiful things of Heaven, and these ladies were sitting in pain and unaware of God's great love for them. Suddenly, God spoke. He said, ***"Are you going to sit on the information you have? Or are you going to do something with it?"*** I of course told the Lord that I would be obedient and do whatever He wanted me to do with it. It was as if He was reminding me that the visions were His and I was holding them back from others and what He wanted to accomplish through them. What happened in the next hour of my life is what you will soon read in the pages of this book. I thought for sure in that moment He would use the visions I had already received in a way He wanted, but He had other plans. God is so great and powerful and the word says in Lamentations 3:22-23 that,

"Because of the Lord's great love we are not consumed, for his compassions never fail. They are new every morning; great is your faithfulness." (NIV).

He had a whole new vision to give me, and that is exactly what He did. As I continued to lay there in my yard, I could feel the Prescence of the Lord hovering over me, and I could feel my spirit opening up. I could feel Heaven and began to get very quiet to receive. the Lord spoke very clearly to me and told me to get up, and go get paper and a pen. I did. Then I came back and as I laid back down, I began to receive the vision of Roses. He told me to write exactly what I heard and saw, and that is exactly what I did. For thirty to forty-five minutes, I wrote as He directed. I was completely caught up in the spirit, and continued to watch this vision unfold before me just like a movie. It was just as if I was walking in the midst of Heaven viewing real-time events. What I witnessed was my little boy Eli, giving a tour of Heaven to a little boy named Isaac. Isaac had just entered Heaven, and Eli had been sent with instructions on where to take him. I saw them walking through Heaven and the different places they visited; like a movie camera following a cast, I followed and took down in the physical what my spiritual eyes were seeing.

I want you to understand dear friend that I wrote this book exactly as the Holy Spirit directed me-word for word. In less than an hour these words flew onto notebook paper and the vision was written. I take no credit for the content of this book. God only used my spiritual eyes, and my physical hand to pen this great work of His enduring love. God allowed me to see my Eli again, assuring me that his life had a place in the beautiful city of Heaven.

I do not know your story, but God does. It is not a coincidence that you have found this book. Whether you have lost a child, a parent, a sibling, a spouse, or any close loved one *God has reserved a meeting with you today in Heaven*. I pray that as you read this story, God begins to plant peace in your heart. A peace that only He can give. If you have had a miscarriage or abortion, do not be afraid.

Your children are not lost, they are waiting!

Before you leave and start your tour of Heaven, I want to tell you I am sorry for your loss. I am sorry your heart has endured this kind of pain. I want to assure you there is hope in Jesus Christ, and He wants you to "...Get up! Pickup your mat and walk." (John 5:8 NIV) and be healed.

Pain in this earthly life is only for a season. The hope of Heaven is REAL. ***JESUS IS REAL*** and your pain is real to Jesus. Give it to Him, and let **HIM HEAL** your heart. We all have a past, but God gives us a bright future through the saving grace of His son **JESUS!**

Remember, even Roses have thorns.

Get up and walk!

-Caroline

Part I
ROSES

Eli- Hi! My name is Eli! Nice to meet you, Isaac!

Isaac- Why are you here Eli?

Eli- I never made it out my Mommy's tummy, but I came straight back to God.

Isaac- Wow! I was really sick on earth, but now look, I am whole!

Eli- That's awesome, being in the presence of Jehovah makes us all new... I've been sent with instructions to give you a tour of Heaven!

Isaac- Really? Where are we going first?

Eli- My favorite part, The Throne Room…

When babies who are never born first arrive in Heaven, they go straight to the Throne room of God.

Isaac- Really?

Eli- Yes. God takes great pride in His children. We are His masterpiece and He takes great pride in giving us our name.

Isaac- You mean God names babies?

Eli- Yes! God gives each one of His special sons and daughters a name when they come back to Heaven.

Isaac- Come back? What do you mean?

Eli- Yes, come back. Some children never make

it out their Mommie's tummy. God's children all originate in Heaven. We each have a purpose on Earth, and in Heaven. Some of our parents send us back to Jesus and some lose us and we come straight back to King Jesus! He's the best, and he is funny too!

Isaac- You mean I get to grow up in Heaven?

Eli- Yes! It's the best place ever, now come with me; we have lots to do and see.

Eli- Our next stop is the nursery. This is where all the babies come when they arrive.

Isaac- Wow! This place is awesome! Who are all these women in the rocking chairs?

Eli- Those are the grandmas! They are grandmas that have been in Heaven a while. They rock their own grandchildren and other grandmas' grandchildren that haven't made it yet. My Great Grandmother rocked me when I first arrived.

Isaac- That's super. What happens when they leave the nursery?

Eli- Great question! We are now traveling to another section of Heaven. The developmental arena!

Isaac- Where are we? There's so many Dads and Moms in here!

Eli- You are right, you are catching on quick! In

Heaven, Dads and Mommies that could never have children on earth have a big role to play in God's city. They help other Mommies' and Daddies' children learn to play and read the Holy Books.

Isaac- Holy Books?

Eli- Yes, stories about God's brave saints that fought for us all to be here.

Isaac- Be here?

Eli- Yes, in Heaven. Some of God's children would have never made it to Heaven if it wasn't for the Saints. They live in a special part of Heaven overlooking the city as a gift from God for their sacrifice. They get to watch their harvest come in every day.

Isaac- Eli, I can't see the end of the row! It looks like it goes on forever!

Jesus- Yes Isaac, you are right it does go on forever…

Isaac- Jesus! Wow is that you! I've seen you once before when I lived on earth.

Jesus- Yes, my son it is I. I have known you your entire life on Earth and now you will live here with me forever.

Isaac- Wow Father you are so beautiful and full of light! Tell me Father, what are these rows and what's growing up out of them?

Jesus- My son, this is my garden of dreams for my children down below on Earth. I plant these dreams in their hearts to fulfill my promises to them. My children that learn to cultivate dominate their life with me at the center. I love my children and want only good for them.

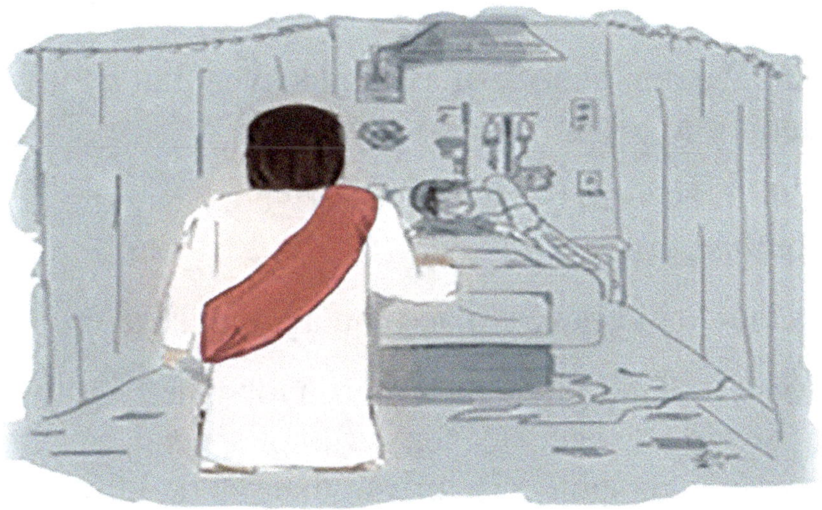

Eli- Isaac, come we must go, the prayer bell is ringing.

Isaac- A prayer bell?

Eli- Yes, in Heaven we spend much time in prayer for our families that are still on Earth. We pray that they will find God and let Him in their hearts when He comes and knocks.

Isaac- Knocks? What does that mean?

Eli- God visits each one of His children below at a designated time in their life. Some answer and let Him in, others turn Him away. Our job is to pray for the time gap in-between that appointed time and when they die; we pray that they will change their mind and let Him in.

Isaac- What happens if they don't change their mind?

Eli- We don't speak of evil in Heaven, but they don't make it up. They go down.

Eli- In Heaven Isaac we are very busy working for the Lord.

Isaac- Will I have a place and a job in Heaven?

Eli- Yes, God gives each of us a job when we arrive in His city. Heaven is full of special sons and daughters living out their eternal life with Jesus. We each live just as we would have on earth except in Heaven we are free from condemnation and fear because of what Jesus did.

Isaac- What did Jesus do?

Eli- Jesus died on Earth so we could all live in Heaven. Isaac, we must hurry, we have great preparation to do.

Isaac- What are you doing now Eli?

Eli- We learn in Heaven to serve others. We must take these rose petals and place them on each one of these path's coming into Heaven! We are preparing for the arrival of some mothers of the special sons and daughters!

Isaac- Why are we placing Rose petals Eli?

Eli- Some Mommies have been very sad on Earth. They have thought that their babies in Heaven would not like them, or not know them.

We must show them lots of love upon their arrival in Heaven. The perfect way to show love is roses. Even though roses have thorns, they create a sweet-smelling flower that is beautiful.

Look Isaac! Here is a Mommie coming now… Isaac looked up and saw a Mommie walking up one of the rose petal paths. She came halfway up the path and stopped. Two little girls came running to her path.

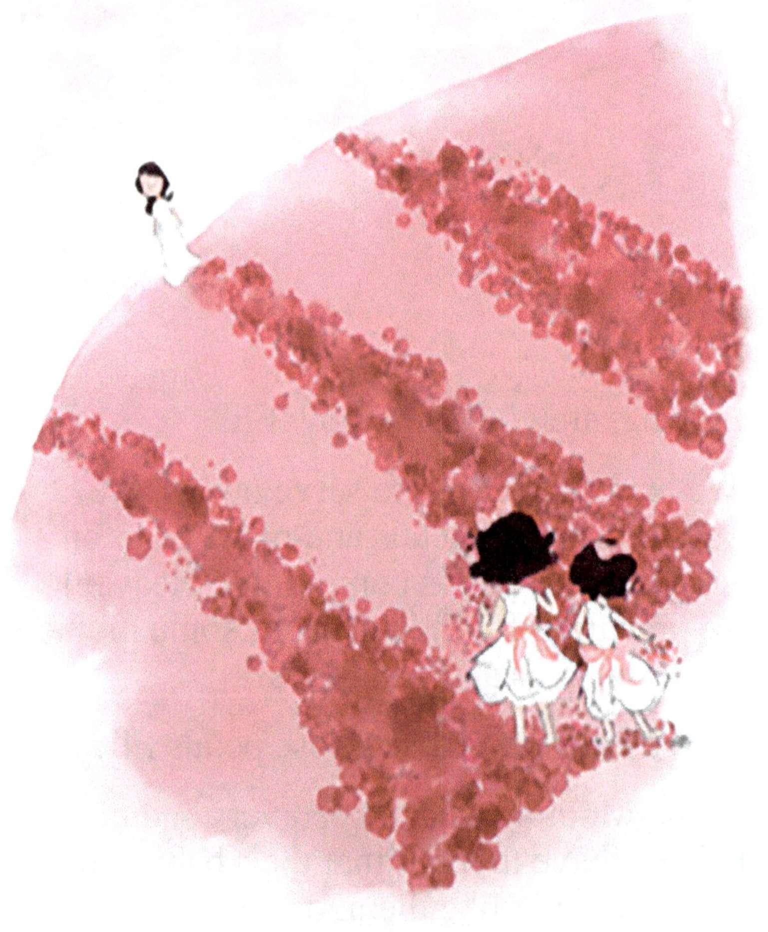

"Mommy! Mommy! We are so glad you are here! We have put many prayers into the prayer bank for you. Now we can live in Heaven together forever."

Isaac- Who are those little girls, Eli?

Eli- That's Izabel and Rebecca. Their Mommie sent them back to Jesus, but look! Aren't you glad she answered the knock!

Isaac- Eli, I have to go pray. My Mommie and Daddy need a knock from God. Thanks for showing me around, I will see ya later!

father God

Please go knock on
my Mommy and daddys
heart. they dont know you
but I do! I have faith
that you can reach their
hearts way down there on
earth. Please knock on
their heart.

Thanks,
your Son
Isaac

PRAYER
BANK

Part II
ROSES

LOOK UP TO HEAVEN

All throughout the word of God we see God's children looking up to Heaven and God speaking to them in miraculous ways. In Matthew chapter 3 we find John the Baptist preaching and baptizing saints of God in the wilderness "preparing the way of the Lord" (Matthew 3:3). John was sent ahead of Jesus to prepare the hearts of the people to receive the real live word of God, walking in the flesh of man, ***Jesus***. At this moment in scripture, we see Jesus, the son of God in human form, coming and asking John to baptize him. As Jesus is baptized by John, we see that all of Heaven ***"opened"*** (Matthew 3:16) and the word tells us that Jesus ***"…saw the Spirit of God descending like a dove, and lighting upon him: And lo a voice from heaven, saying, This is my beloved Son, in whom I am well pleased." (Matthew 3:16-17 KJV).***

Can you imagine the Savior of the world who came from Heaven, and walked closer with Father God than any human, could have this experience of Heaven being opened unto him? Why couldn't he just have looked into Heaven on his own? Because even though Jesus was fully God, he was fully human; and while he was here on earth, he experienced Heaven the same way that you and I do, through the Spirit of God. In our own strength we can never reach Heaven. You could spend billions of dollars to take a trip to space and search for the portal to Heaven and you would fail. Why? Because you are human. Just as Jesus faced physical limitations during His earthly life, so do you. This is the problem that we all face as humans; how do we attain Heaven? What must we do to walk into the Glory of God one day and live in eternal bliss? The hard truth is that you could spend your whole life working towards heaven and doing all the right things and at the end of your life you would still not be prepared to meet your maker God. ***In our own strength we can*** *do nothing.* Here is the good news for you and I; because Jesus was born from Heaven, through the womb of his Mother Mary into earth, we can ascend into glory at the end of our earthly life because *He gave His earthly life in our place.*

TAKE HEAVEN BY FAITH

I am sure that the reason you have read this book is because you have a loved one in Heaven. Maybe you are curious about Heaven? The vision that I wrote in this book was a beautiful gift from God given through The Holy Spirit. In obedience to my father God, I have now shared it with you. We must move when God takes action in our lives. He shares Heaven with us through His Son Jesus Christ, so that we can all share Heaven with Him in eternity. *How do you take Heaven by faith*? By believing Jesus Christ came to earth through the womb of a virgin, was born and lived a sinless life, and was crucified not for his sin, but ours. Jesus hung on the cross at Calvary that fateful day to prepare a staircase to Heaven that can only be climbed in faith. Romans 4:25 assures us that, **"He (Jesus) was delivered over to death for our sins and was raised to life for our justification." (NIV).** So now, knowing that Jesus was given in our place on the cross to cover our sins, let us continue reading the word together again in Romans 10:9-13.

> **"If you declare with your mouth, "Jesus is Lord," and believe in your heart that God raised him from the dead, you will be saved. For it is with your heart that you believe and are justified, and it is with your mouth that you profess your faith and are saved. As Scripture says, "Anyone who believes in him will never be put to shame." For there is no difference between Jew and Gentile—the same Lord is Lord of all and richly blesses all who call on him, for, "Everyone who calls on the name of the Lord will be saved." NIV.**

Jesus lived a sinless life, died, was crucified, and buried. Three days later He rose again holding the keys to Hell and the grave annihilating Satan's power over God's creation. You must *confess* with your mouth that you are a sinner and *repent* of your sins. The moment that *you believe and confess that Jesus is Lord,* all of Heaven and its glory is opened to you through the filling of The Holy Spirit; into your soul and becomes your eternal home immediately no matter how long you live on this earth. What a glorious promise!

At the moment of surrender to Jesus by faith, the hope of Heaven is deposited in your heart opening the stairway for your spirit to access Heaven and all it holds. Yes! Read that again, the *MOMENT* you surrender and believe by faith that Jesus is the atonement for your sin, ALL OF HEAVEN IS OPENED TO YOU!!!! This is such an exciting revelation and as you begin to rest in this promise your life will never be the same. God confirms this hope in His living word in the book of Colossians. I encourage you to read the entire book of Romans and Colossians on your own, but for now, we will look at Colossians 1:5-6 together,

> **"the faith and love that spring from the hope stored up for you in heaven and about which you have already heard in the true message of the gospel that has come to you. In the same way, the gospel is bearing fruit and growing throughout the whole world—just as it has been doing among you since the day you heard it and truly understood God's grace." NIV**

Jesus is the living word of God, deposited in us by faith. Bringing a whole new realm of life and spiritual gifts into existence for us. Heaven not only becomes our eternal home, but a place we visit by our spirit, through the eyes of the Holy Spirit of God.

The hope of Heaven is Jesus, and when we believe in Him, "we become one with Him" (Galatians 3:27-28). Jesus tells us in John 14:23,

> *"Jesus answered, "If anyone loves me, he will keep my word. My Father will love him, and we will come to him and make our home with him." (CSB)*

Our time together here on these pages is almost over, but I have a few more things to tell you before you go. God is building a foundation of faith for you to receive your own blessings from The Holy Spirit. You must read the word of God for yourself daily and search the scriptures and God will reveal Himself to you in a very personal way.

Look now with me to 1 Peter 1:3-4:

> ***"Blessed be the God and Father of our Lord Jesus Christ. Because of his great mercy he has given us new birth into a living hope through the resurrection of Jesus Christ from the dead and into an inheritance that is imperishable, undefiled, and unfading, kept in heaven for you." CSB***

Jesus Christ is alive and He is *"sitting at the right hand of the Father" (Luke 22:69)*. He is your hope in Heaven and the anchor of your ship. He is the inheritance in Heaven that will never change just as the scripture in 1 Peter says. By faith, you must believe. Heaven is real, and so are your ties to it as a believer in Jesus Christ. Christ has literally tied himself to you from Heaven, and you will never be cut off if you believe.

Reading further in 1 Peter 1:8-9 it gives us this great hope,

> ***"Though you have not seen him, you love him; and even though you do not see him now, you believe in him and are filled with an inexpressible and glorious joy, for you are receiving the end result of your faith, the salvation of your souls." NIV***

As a believer in Christ, you already have the end result, (the salvation of your soul (1 Peter 1:9)) … Jesus Christ gives us as believers the faith to take Heaven and all it offers by faith. Now, one last stop before the end of our journey through the word together.

FEAR KILLS- FAITH FLIES

When we lose someone to death it is a scary and unknown experience. If you have, you know exactly what I am talking about. The feelings of anger, resentment, fear, helplessness, and loss cloud around us when we lose a loved one. As you have read over the last few paragraphs, Jesus defeated all those things at the cross. He took all those things on the cross so when the time came for us to face them, *He already had* and conquered them. As someone who has experienced loss first hand, Jesus was the only one who could help me. Others around me had no idea the depth of pain I physically felt, or mentally endured. I am writing all this for a reason. To encourage and help you see that Jesus is the answer to all these things. After all these years, I still have bad days, but when I do, I go into the secret place with God, and **He comforts me with the hope of Heaven;** *His Son, Jesus Christ*. I know that my baby and loved ones are in Heaven, and that is the comfort that I need. The grace I need to continue walking out my earthly life with purpose is the assurance that I will one day be reunited with all my loved ones for eternity. There is no fear in Heaven, only faith.

Jesus loves you and the word says in 1 John 4:18 that:

> *"There is no fear in love. But perfect love drives out fear, because fear has to do with punishment. The one who fears is not made perfect in love." NIV.*

Jesus drives the fear out of our hearts because his love was perfect, missing nothing that we need, or will need. He fills us with living water and makes us new.

ITS YOUR TURN NOW

At this time, I must ask you a question?

Where are you headed friend?

Imagine you are standing in the middle of nowhere and there are two roads; one leading to the hope of Heaven, and the other leading straight to Hell? I have shared with you a very personal encounter. It took years for me to even share this with anyone because it was so raw and special to me. Why would I do this you may ask? ***I believe God gave me this vision not just for my own comfort, but for yours.*** I know where I am headed, but do you? I have shared my vision of Heaven, and we have walked through the word of God together. This is where I must exit the ride and let you finish it by yourself. You are never alone with God. Take some time now to answer these questions for yourself. Are you ready to meet God? Has the Blood of Christ been applied to your sins? If you are a believer in Jesus Christ, I pray this story and time together in the word has strengthened and opened your eyes in a new way to the depths of the Father's love for you and the many ways He is willing to reach down from Heaven and comfort His children. Even something as small as this book being written, was nothing short of God's great arm of love reaching down to comfort and love me, and you. If you are not a believer in Jesus Christ, and cannot say for certain that the gates of Heaven will be opened for you, I pray that you will seek the Lord, confess your sins, and submit your life to Him. In the following pages there are resources to help you make this decision. Do not spend eternity in Hell. Answer the knock of God on your heart's door today and let Him in.

I must leave you now, go in peace and seek for yourself the great and glorious gates of glory found only through the Blood of Jesus Christ.

God speed,

JCR

If you are ready to accept Jesus as your Lord and Savior, pray this simple prayer as you submit yourself fully to Him and His purpose for your life.

Father God,

I come to you a sinner, knowing my life's position is not where it needs to be. I confess my sins before you now, and ask you to come and cleanse me from all unrighteousness, with the Blood of your Son Jesus Christ. Wash me now and make me clean. I give my life to you, take it, and do something with it. Help me to lay down all my burdens at the feet of my Savior Jesus Christ and never pick them up again. I need you, Father. I want a relationship with you above all else. Help me I pray, to renew my mind, and body and make me a new creature in Christ Jesus. I love you Father, I receive your precious Holy Spirit in my spirit that you gave me to communicate with you. Teach me Holy Spirit and guide me into all truth by the word of God. I believe that Jesus Christ has secured my hope in Heaven by His blood, and I take Heaven and all it offers me now by faith. I plead the blood of Jesus over my life, and go in peace… in Jesus's name I pray, Amen.

Today is a new day, and one you will never forget. Sign your name for the first time as a new citizen of Heaven washed in The Blood of Jesus Christ your Lord!

Name: ____

Date of new birth: _____________________________________

Now, go, and testify to the great love of God in your life. You are forever tied to Heaven through the saving blood of Jesus Christ!

John 14:6-7;

> **"Jesus answered, "I am the way and the truth and the life. No one comes to the Father except through me. If you really know me, you will know my father as well. From now on, you do know him and have seen him." NIV**

FULLY RESTORED

ABOUT THE AUTHOR

Caroline plays the piano, guitar, and sings most every day. She has written many songs about Heaven, her children, and her own personal life. Singles such as, **"The Babies of Heaven," "Hebron," "Sing Over Me Carolina," "Tears & Thorns,"** and many more. You can hear some of her music on her website which is listed in the reference section of the book.

This part of the book serves as a memorial to God and all He has done in her life. Caroline is now remarried, and living out the beautiful grace of God, with her husband Brent, and son John Thomas. She owns and operates two businesses, and is very involved in her community. Caroline is available for speaking and singing engagements by request. She loves her Lord, her husband, her children, and her Country.

Caroline is a South Carolinian by birth, and a citizen of Heaven by the Blood of Jesus Christ.

In Loving Memory

John 14:1-4 NIV

"Do not let your hearts be troubled. You believe in God; believe also in me. My Father's house has many rooms; if that were not so, would I have told you that I am going there to prepare a place for you? And if I go and prepare a place for you, I will come back and take you to be with me that you also may be where I am. You know the way to the place where I am going."

SETH GARNER SQUIRES

ELI SQUIRES

"I can almost see the gates"

"Just over there beyond those hills,

Lies a dream that is never fulfilled,

Without a man who walked this earth,

And told of His virgin birth,

A man who came for all you see,

To save a wretched sinner like me,

Just over there beyond those hills,

Lies a dream He came to give."

Caroline Richardson 2024

RESOURCES & CONTACT INFORMATION

IF you have made a decision to accept Jesus as your Lord and Savior today, find a local church where they can help you grow as a new believer in Christ. If you need help finding one, reach out to the email provided below and ask for help. Never stop telling the good news of Jesus!!

If you are looking for a place to donate in honor of your loved one, below are two great ministries that have personally impacted my life in an eternal way. Thank you for reading ROSES, and I pray that this book will have an eternal impact on your life, and the life of others. When you donate to these ministries, you will be planting a seed of LIFE into a beautiful soul you will one day meet at the gates of Heaven.

Always in faith

Caroline

Coastline Women's Center
coastlinewomenscenter.org

Hebron Colony Ministries
hebroncolony.org

ARTIST RECOGITION

Abbi Meckley

Roses has been years in the making. When I wrote the vision from Heaven in the spring of 2022, the Lord instructed me in specific places where there was to be an illustration in the vision. He also instructed me as to who would illustrate them. ***Abbi Meckley just happens to be my sister!*** I knew that the Holy Spirit would give her, when the time was right, the ability to draw in the physical what I saw in the spiritual. The Lord never disappoints! With very little detail given, Abbi was able to be led by the Holy Spirit and visualize almost exactly every detail of what I saw in Heaven on the pages of ***Roses***. This is nothing short of the miracle working power of God, and He gets *ALL* the credit. I love my sister dearly and I am so proud of her accomplishments as an artist, writer, and most importantly, a daughter of the King. The kingdom work of ***Roses*** would not be complete without her. I love you Abbi!

Abbi lives in the low country of South Carolina along with her husband and 3 children. She draws inspiration from her family and friends around her. Her style has been called "whimsical" and "childlike" and that is ok with her. She believes that we can trust God best when we come to Him as a child.

Abbi is an accomplished illustrator and writer. She has illustrated many beautiful works for individuals, businesses, and commercial print. Her talent is God-given and it shows. Her work depicts the innocence of life through the eyes of a pure believer.

Ann Turner

I met Ann Turner in late summer of 2023. Ann was introduced to me by Jeannie Scott Smith who was instrumental in making Roses come to life. Ann had worked with Jeannie on many of her own publications such as, ***"The Gift"***. Jeannie asked me if she could share ***ROSES*** with Ann, and I told her yes.

After reading, Ann and I talked for a good while on the telephone one day and I shared with her my testimony and the story behind ROSES. Ann was able to take the vision and create a beautiful cover that fills me with joy. Every person that looks at this cover will begin to look up to Heaven and seek the Lord.

Ann was given the scripture on the cover by the Holy Spirit, ***"I Am The Rose of Sharon"*** which is found in Song of Solomon 2. This scripture sets a precedence letting readers know this book is about the awe-inspiring love of God at work in the lives of His dear children. Ann is a true saint of God. She will receive a reward one day in Heaven she will never be able to imagine, for her obedience in her earthly life, and her work in the building of God's great and glorious kingdom.

Speaking Engagements:

If you would like to schedule Caroline to sing or speak at an event, please email her at: junecrichardson@proton.me

Thank you for reading ROSES!

You can learn more about the author online at: www. juneia.org